BY VALERIE BODDEN

CREATIVE EDUCATION

Published by Creative Education
P.O. Box 227, Mankato, Minnesota 56002
Creative Education is an imprint of The Creative Company
www.thecreativecompany.us

Design and production by The Design Lab
Art direction by Rita Marshall
Printed in the United States of America

Photographs by Alamy (Chad Ehlers) Corbis (Bettmann, Richard
Bickel, Roger De La Harpe/Gallo Images, Peter Johnson, Charles
& Josette Lenars, Ludovic Maisant, Galen Rowell, Paul A. Souders,
Nik Wheeler), Dreamstime (Ecophoto, Naturepix), Getty Images
(MACKSON WASAMUNU/AFP), iStockphoto (Lance Bellers)

Copyright © 2010 Creative Education
International copyright reserved in all countries. No
part of this book may be reproduced in any form
without written permission from the publisher.

Library of Congress Cataloging-in-Publication Data
Bodden, Valerie.
Victoria Falls / by Valerie Bodden.
p. cm. — (Big outdoors)
Summary: A fundamental introduction to Victoria Falls, including
the river and forests that surround it, the creatures that live near
it, and how people have affected its rugged environment.
Includes index.
ISBN 978-1-58341-819-2
1. Victoria Falls (Zambia and Zimbabwe)—
Juvenile literature. I. Title. II. Series.

DT3140.V54B63 2010
968.91—dc22   2009004692

9 8 7 6 5 4 3 2

BIG OUTDOORS
VICTORIA FALLS

AFRICA

Victoria Falls is one of the biggest waterfalls in the world. It is on the **continent** of Africa. It is on the Zambezi River between the countries of Zambia and Zimbabwe (*zim-BOB-way*).

A bridge close to the Falls goes from Zambia to Zimbabwe

Victoria Falls is made up of five waterfalls separated by small islands.

Rainbows can often
be seen in the spray
above Victoria Falls.

Victoria Falls is more than
one mile (1.6 km) wide.
Water falls 350 feet (105
m) from the top of the
waterfall to the river below.
The crashing water makes
clouds of white spray go up
in the air.

Sunlight that bounces off the spray makes rainbows

Scientists think that Victoria Falls was formed after a big crack opened in the earth. The Zambezi River began to fall over the crack, forming a waterfall. Over time, the falling water wore the edge of the waterfall away. The new edge of the waterfall was farther up the river. This happened many times.

The crack in the earth that made the Falls is called a gorge

The water from Victoria Falls could fill 100 swimming pools in 1 minute!

The weather around Victoria Falls is hot and rainy in the summer. It is warm and dry in the winter. There are towns on each side of the waterfall.

People can stay at hotels (above) when they visit the Falls

Crocodiles and hippos rest in the Zambezi River above Victoria Falls. Zebras, elephants, and giraffes roam the land next to the river. Baobab (*BAY-oh-bab*), sausage, and palm trees grow nearby.

Baobab trees (above) and elephants (opposite) are found nearby

There is a forest on the warm, wet cliffs across from Victoria Falls. Fig and ebony trees grow in the forest. Monkeys, warthogs, and black eagles live there.

Warthogs (opposite) and monkeys (above) are African animals

Native peoples used to **worship** at Victoria Falls. The first white people saw Victoria Falls about 150 years ago. They named it after Queen Victoria of England. Victoria Falls became a popular place to visit about 20 years ago.

In the 1850s, the Falls were named for Victoria (opposite)

VICTORIA FALLS **17** BIG OUTDOORS

Some native people call Victoria Falls "The Smoke That Thunders."

Visitors have not had a big effect on Victoria Falls yet. But some people worry that visitors could **pollute** the water near Victoria Falls. Climbers could wear away the dirt and rocks of cliffs, too.

Only a small fence stands between people and the Falls

Many people who visit Victoria Falls get to the other side of the waterfall by train. Some raft through the **rapids** below the waterfall. But most people just stand and stare at this amazing wall of water!

People who stand across from the Falls can get a close-up look

The rumble from Victoria Falls can be heard 20 miles (32 km) away!

21

Some people like to bungee jump
from the Victoria Falls bridge.

Glossary

continent one of Earth's seven big pieces of land

native original; native peoples were the first to live in an area

pollute to make dirty with chemicals or other things that are bad for the earth, water, or air

rapids parts of rivers that are fast and rough

worship to pray and do things for a god

Read More about It

Fowler, Allan. *The Wonder of a Waterfall.* New York: Children's Press, 1999.

Haskins, James, and Kathleen Benson. *Count Your Way through Zimbabwe.* Minneapolis: Millbrook Press, 2007.

Index

UNION COUNTY PUBLIC LIBRARY
316 E. Windsor St., Monroe, N.C. 28112

3-13